My Picture Dictionary

by Hale C. Reid
Helen W. Crane

Ginn and Company
A Xerox Education Company

Aa Bb Cc Dd

Ee Ff Gg Hh

Ii Jj Kk Ll

Mm Nn Oo Pp

Qq Rr Ss Tt

Uu Vv Ww Xx

Yy Zz

Home Office, Lexington, Massachusetts 02173
0-663-31522-0

A a

airport

apple

a

about

across

after

again

all

always

am

an

and

another

any

are

around

as

asked

at

ate

away

Bb

baby

baseball

bag

basket

bear

ball

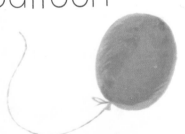

balloon

bed

barn

bee

4

B b

bell

book

bicycle

box

bird

boys

birthday

bread

boat

brook

B b

bug

bunny

bus

button

back

be

because

best

better

big

bite

bring

build

bump

but

buy

buzzed

by

C c

cake

chair

candle

chicks

candy

children

car

circus

cat

clock

C c

clown

coat

cookies

corn

cowboy

call

came

can

can't

catch

city

cold

color

come

coming

could

crying

8

Dd

dog

doll

dress

duck

day
did
didn't
dinner
do
don't
down
drop

Ee

eggs

eat

every

9

F f

farm

flowers

father

feather

fire

fish

fast
faster
find
for
found
friend
frisky
from
fun
funny

G g

girls

goat

grandfather

grandmother

groceries

game
gave
get
getting
give
go
going
gone
good
good-by
got
guess

11

Hh

hamburger

hen

hand

hill

hat

heart

home

helicopter

honey

horn

12

horse

house

had

happen

happy

has

have

he

hear

heard

hello

help

her

here

hide

him

his

hot

how

hurry

I i

ice

ice cream

iron

I
if
I'm
in
into
is
it

J j

jeep

jet

jingle

job

jump

just

14

K k

key

kitten

king

knife

kitchen

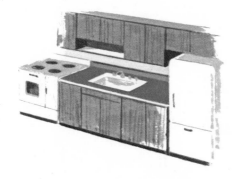

| keep |
| kept |
| kind |
| knew |
| knock |
| know |

kite

L l

lamb

leaves

letter

lion

lunch

laughed
learn
let
let's
like
little
live
long
look
lost
lot
love

Mm

mailbox

money

man

moon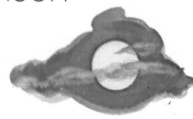

mother

meat

milk

mitten

mountain

Mm

mouse

machine
made
make
many
may
maybe
me
men
met

middle
might
mill
miss
more
morning
most
Mr.
Mrs.
much
must
my

Nn

nail

nest

newspaper

nickel

nuts

name
need
never
new
next
nice
night
no
noise
not
nothing
now

O o

ocean

orange

owl

o'clock

of

off

often

oh

old

on

once

only

open

or

other

our

out

over

own

Pp

pan

pennies

pancakes

people

paper

pets

park

picnic

pencil

P p

pocket

pole

policeman

pony

postman

puppy

paint

party

plant

play

please

pop

pretty

puddle

put

quarter

queen

| quack |
| question |
| quick |
| quiet |

rabbit

rain

rooster

| race |
| ran |
| ready |
| ride |
| ring |
| rolled |
| run |

S s

saddle

seesaw

Santa Claus

sheep

satellite

shoe

school

skate

scissors

sky

S s

sled

squirrel

snake

star

snow

store

snowman

street

sprinkler

streetcar

S s

sun

said	sleep
sang	so
sat	some
saw	something
say	soon
see	splash
shall	started
she	stay
side	step
sing	stop
	story
	surprise

Tt

table

television

taxi

top

teacher

town

teeth

toys

telephone

tractor

27

T t

train

tree

truck

turkey

turtle

take
than
thank
that
the
their
them
then
there
they
thing
think

this
three
time
tiny
to

today
tomorrow
too
took
two

umbrella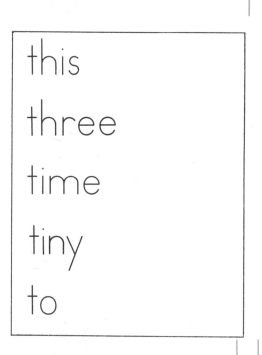

up
us

valentine

very
visiting

W w

wagon

watch

wheat

wheel

whistle

window

wolf

woman

woods

world

W w

wait	what
walk	when
want	where
warm	who
was	will
wash	win
water	wish
way	with
we	wonderful
well	word
went	work
were	would

X x

xylophone

x as in:

box

fox

Y y

yard

yes

you

your

Z z

zoo

zero

zoom

Action Words

climb   hop   run

swim   swing

skip   dance   walk

jump   skate

Parts of the Body

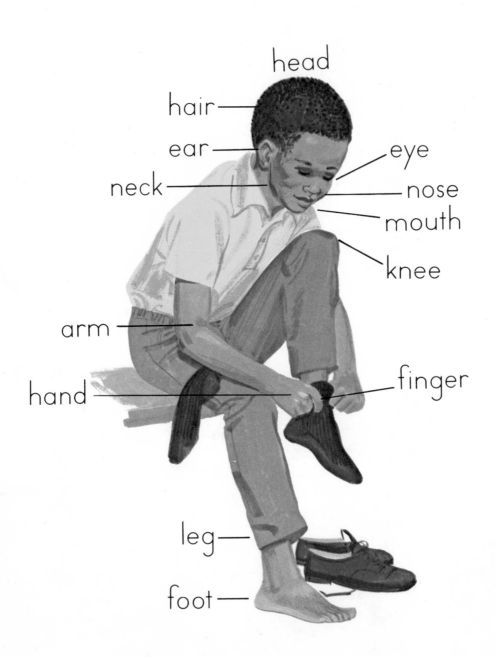

head

hair

ear

neck

eye

nose

mouth

knee

arm

hand

finger

leg

foot

The Family

mother   father

sister

baby

brother

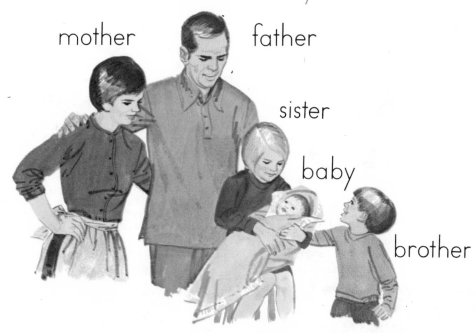

cousins   aunt   uncle

grandmother

grandfather

Toys

doll   kite   drum

train   ball

car   truck   boat

wagon   bicycle

Helpful Little Words

across

between

into

on

up

in   out

down

over

under

Farm

haystack

tractor

silo

barn

farmhouse

pump

pigs

fence

garden

grass

cow

calf

chickens

pony

City

buildings

apartments

traffic light

department store

hotel

bank

post office

policeman

car

bus

mailbox

street

fire hydrant

sidewalk

Fruits

plum   orange   lemon

banana   grapes

cherry   pear   apple

strawberry   peach

Vegetables

potato   peas   onion

celery   squash

beans   beet   cabbage

lettuce   carrot

Weather

moon   stars   sun

snow   sky

wind   clouds   rain

lightning   rainbow

Kinds of Workers

farmer

fire fighter

dentist

police officer

bus driver

teacher

doctor

mail carrier

Animals

rabbit  bear  monkey

fox  raccoon

elephant  seal  tiger

lion  beaver

Number Zoo

1 one

2 two

3 three

4 four

5 five

6 six

7 seven

8 eight

9 nine

10 ten

Days of the Week

Sunday
Monday
Tuesday
Wednesday
Thursday
Friday
Saturday

Colors

yellow   green   blue   orange

red   brown   white   black

Months and Holidays

January	February	March
New Year's Day 	Valentine's Day 	

April	May	June
	Mother's Day 	Father's Day 

July	August	September
 Fourth of July		

October	November	December
Halloween 	Thanksgiving Day 	Christmas Day 

47

ILLUSTRATIONS BY ROBERT CARDEN

My Picture Dictionary is designed to help the small child help himself in writing and spelling. It also introduces the dictionary habit, which can and should be encouraged as early as the First Grade. As children use the illustrations to locate words in this simple dictionary, they learn that words (1) have printed symbols and (2) can be arranged alphabetically. Usually this experience is their first contact with words in an alphabetical arrangement.

Selection of Content

The 175 nouns illustrated in this dictionary were selected from 2800 different words found in 4500 independently written compositions of 1500 first-grade children. The additional 272 words in the body of the dictionary are among those which appeared with the highest frequencies in these compositions. The entire word list has been closely correlated with the vocabulary of the early books in the Reading 360 Program, as well as the GINN BASIC READING SERIES.

Included in this dictionary are also sixteen classification pages of pictured words such as "Toys," "Fruits," and "Animals." These pages add 132 more words to the dictionary.

Format

The pictured words are listed first under each guide letter. The words that do not lend themselves to illustration are alphabetized separately in easily distinguishable columns.

The entries are in manuscript writing such as the child will be learning and using. The single-word entry makes it easy for the first- or second-grade child to find the words he needs in his early composition work. Guide letters, both capital and small, help the child locate the word he wants to write.

The illustrations appear below or beside the entry words. Their simplicity helps a pupil acquire precise meanings.

Suggestions for Helping Children

When a child asks for the spelling of a word, help him to identify the initial letter, as *b* in *boat*. Then help him to find the pages on which the words beginning with that letter are pictured.

Using the dictionary to find out how words are spelled will help him recognize that words beginning with the same sound often start with the same letter.

Although it is not necessary for a child to know the alphabet to look up a word, he will soon learn it through constant use.

The use of *My Picture Dictionary* enables pupils to progress at their own speed in writing activities and thus helps the teacher to provide for individual needs and abilities.

ABCDEFGH 08107987

PRINTED IN THE UNITED STATES OF AMERICA